🌲 Crabtree Publishing C

www.crabtreebooks.com

D1360051

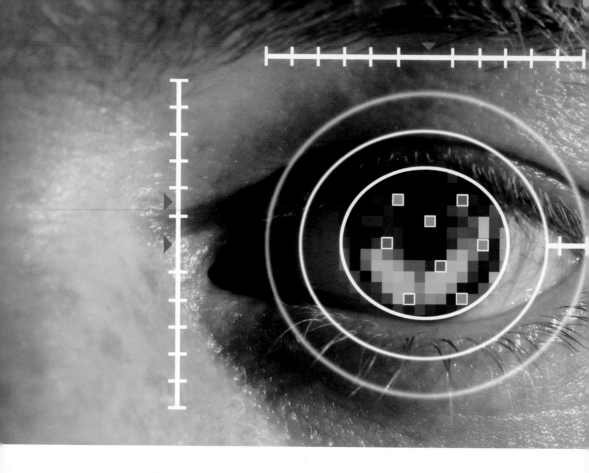

## Crabtree Publishing Company

www.crabtreebooks.com          1-800-387-7650

PMB 59051                      616 Welland Avenue,
350 Fifth Avenue, 59th Floor   St. Catharines, Ontario
New York, NY, 10118            L2M 5V6

Content development by         Published by
Shakespeare Squared            Crabtree Publishing
                               Company © 2010
www.ShakespeareSquared.com
                               First published

in Great Britain in
2010 by TickTock
Entertainment Ltd.

Printed in the
U.S.A./122009
CG20091120

Crabtree Publishing
Company credits:
Project manager: Kathy Middleton
Editor: Reagan Miller
Production coordinator: Katherine Berti
Prepress technician: Katherine Berti

TickTock credits:
Publisher: Melissa Fairley
Art director: Faith Booker
Editor: Victoria Garrard
Designer: Emma Randall
Production controller: Ed Green
Production manager: Suzy Kelly

Thank you to Lorraine Petersen and the members of nasen

Picture credits (t=top; b=bottom; c=centre; l=left; r=right; OFC=outside front cover;
OBC=outside): AFP/Getty Images: 28–29. Andrew Brookes, National Physical Laboratory/
Science Photo Library: 12b. Corbis/SuperStock: 15b. Courtesy of AeroVironment, Inc.: 21
Courtesy of Emue Technologies: 23b. Ed Darack/Science Faction/Corbis: 9b. Getty Imag
5b, 8, 16, 17t, 20–21. John Giles/PA Archive/Press Association Images: 19t. iStock: OFCl,
OFC (background), 5t, 6, OBCr, OBC (background). James King-Holmes/Science Photo
Library: 10. Kim Kulish/Corbis: 17b. Frans Lanting/Corbis: 13b. Pablo Paul/Alamy: 15t.
Shutterstock: OFCtl, OFCbl, 1, 2, 4, 7t, 9t, 11, 12–13, 14, 18–19, 22, 23t, 24, 25, 26–27t
OBCtr, OBCl. Time & Life Pictures/Getty Images: 26–27. www.janespencer.com: 7b.

Every effort has been made to trace copyright holders, and we apologize in advance
for any omissions. We would be pleased to insert the appropriate acknowledgments
in any subsequent edition of this publication.

**Library and Archives Canada Cataloguing in Publication**

Hubbard, Ben
      Hi tech world : high level security / Ben Hubbard.


(Crabtree contact)
Includes index.
ISBN 978-0-7787-7530-0 (bound).--ISBN 978-0-7787-7552-2 (pbk.)


      1. Electronic surveillance--Juvenile literature.  2. Security
systems--Juvenile literature.  I. Title.  II. Series: Crabtree contact

TK7882.E2H82 2010        j621.389'28        C2009-906792-7

**Library of Congress Cataloging-in-Publication Data**

Hubbard, Ben.
   Hi tech world : high level security / Ben Hubbard.
      p. cm. -- (Crabtree contact)
   Includes index.
   ISBN 978-0-7787-7552-2 (pbk. : alk. paper)
   -- ISBN 978-0-7787-7530-0 (lib. bdg. : alk. paper)
   1.  Electronic surveillance--Juvenile literature. 2.  Security systems--
Juvenile literature. I. Title.

   TK7882.E2H83 2010
   005.8--dc22

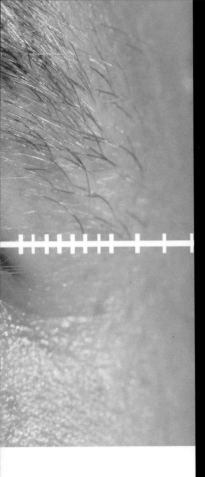

*Iris recognition scan*

# CONTENTS

# INTRODUCTION

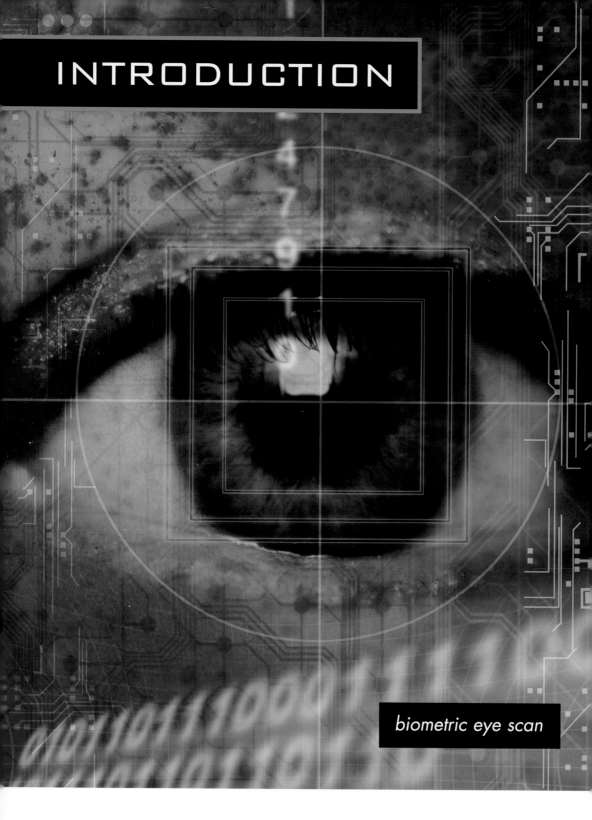

biometric eye scan

The modern world is all about technology. Technology makes our lives easier and safer. But how does it do this?

**CCTV (closed-circuit television)** *monitors*

*spy plane*

The following pages explain the latest and greatest technology, from modern security in the home to **biometrics** and hi-tech spy planes.

# HOME SECURITY

In medieval times, castles protected the people inside with moats, drawbridges, and huge iron gates.

In the early 1900s, the first burglar alarms were installed in homes in New York City.

Today, we rely on technology to keep our homes secure. Home security systems use keypad entry, **motion sensors**, and CCTV cameras.

*a keypad entry system*

We can now control our security systems from cell phones, using a **Web browser**. This means we can watch what is going on inside our homes from anywhere in the world!

# PANIC ROOMS

**Homes owned by wealthy people sometimes contain secret panic rooms.**

Often hidden in the basement, these rooms are built from reinforced concrete with blast-proof steel doors.

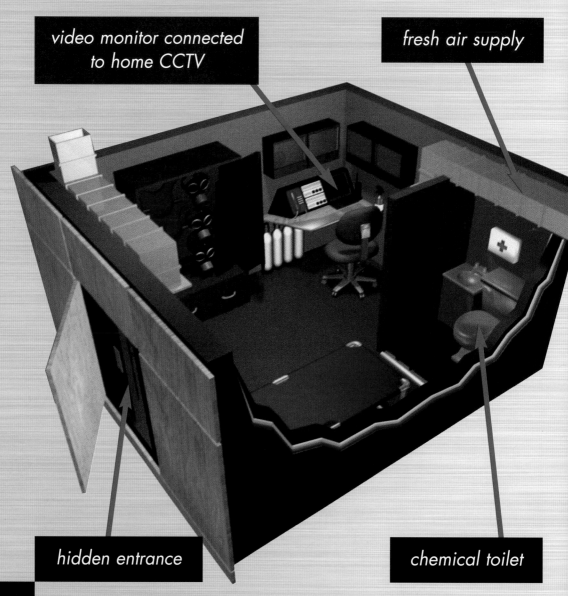

video monitor connected to home CCTV

fresh air supply

hidden entrance

chemical toilet

A basic panic room consists of a small room with a solid door and dead-bolt lock.

More expensive panic rooms use high-strength glass. This glass does not shatter when hit with great force.

# BIOMETRICS

**Biometrics is like your own PIN (personal identification number) that nobody else can steal.**

It works by recording a physical feature only you have, such as your fingerprints. This recording becomes your own unique password. But unlike a password, you cannot ever forget your fingerprints, and no one can steal your fingerprints. People use biometric technology to protect computer files and other private information.

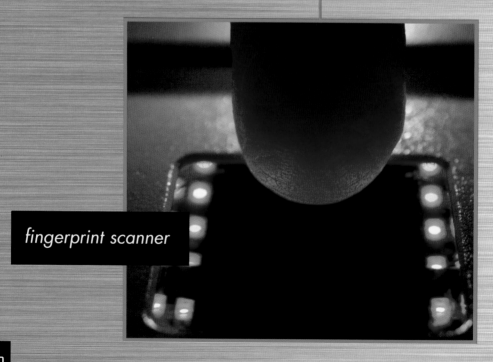

*fingerprint scanner*

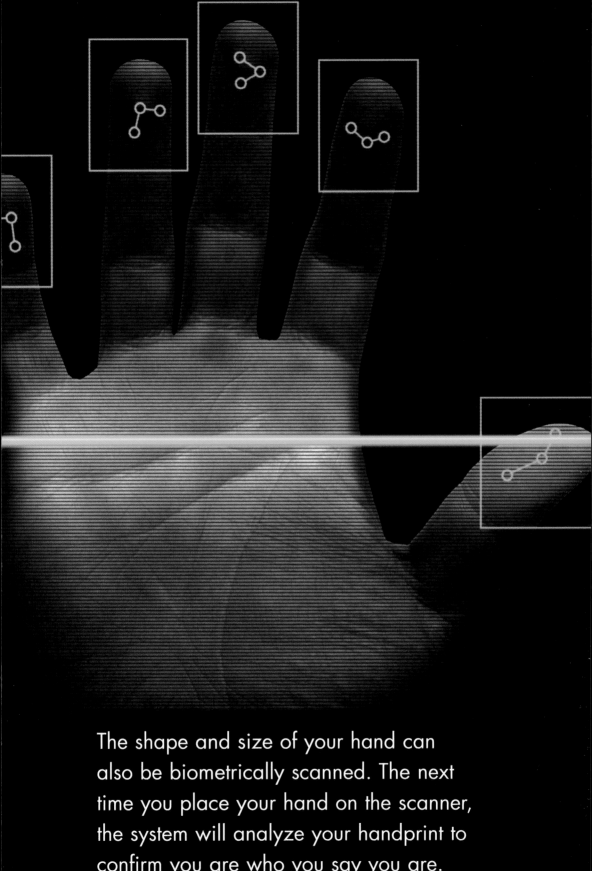

The shape and size of your hand can also be biometrically scanned. The next time you place your hand on the scanner, the system will analyze your handprint to confirm you are who you say you are.

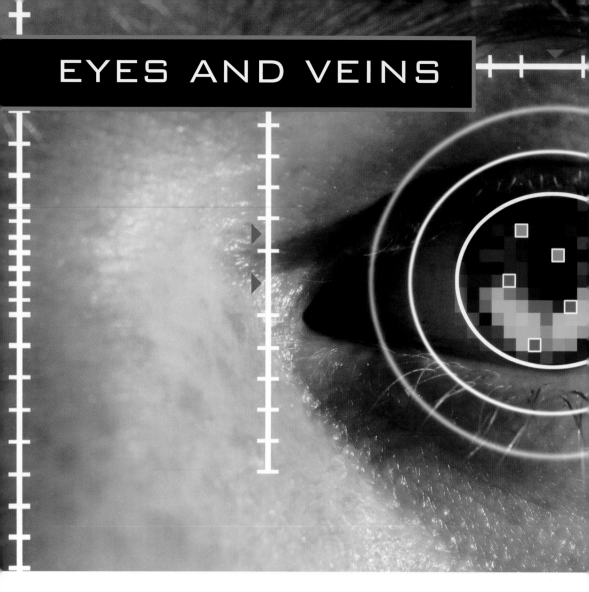

## Iris recognition

A camera takes a photo of your iris—the colored ring around the pupil in your eye. This is the most reliable biometric technology, because people's eyes do not change over time.

*iris recognition scanner*

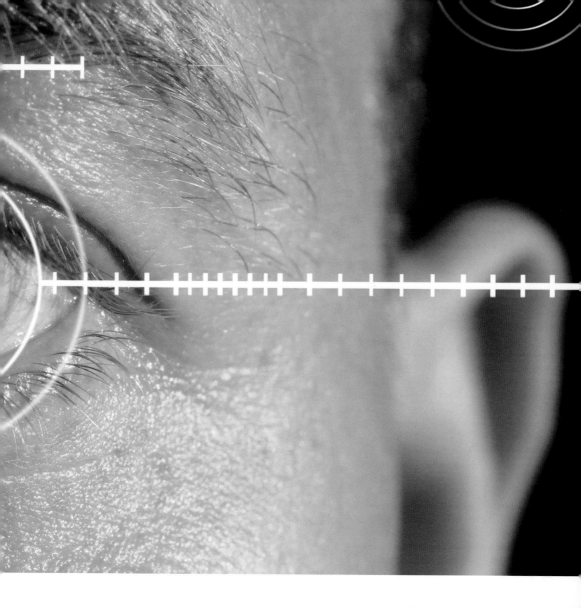

## Vein scanning

A camera takes a picture of your wrist, finger, or palm using **infrared** light. This light makes the blood in your veins appear black. The camera then records and stores the unique map of your veins.

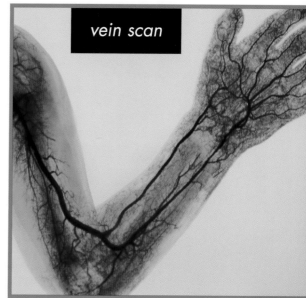

*vein scan*

# AIRPORTS

**Every year, more than 1.5 billion people travel by airplane. Each of these passengers and their bags are checked for guns and explosives.**

*Luggage is searched at an airport.*

## Paperless tickets

Passengers download electronic tickets to their cell phones. The e-tickets are then scanned at the airport.

## Passports

Most passports now contain a biometric chip. The chip contains information that is unique to you, such as the distance between your eyes. This information helps prevent someone from using another person's passport.

biometric chip

## Metal detectors

Every passenger has to pass through a metal detector. Hand-held metal detectors can locate exactly where a metal object is.

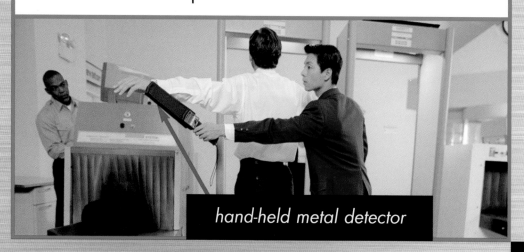

hand-held metal detector

## X-ray machines

These machines scan your luggage and display the objects inside by shape and color. For example, all metal objects are shown in the same color on the scan.

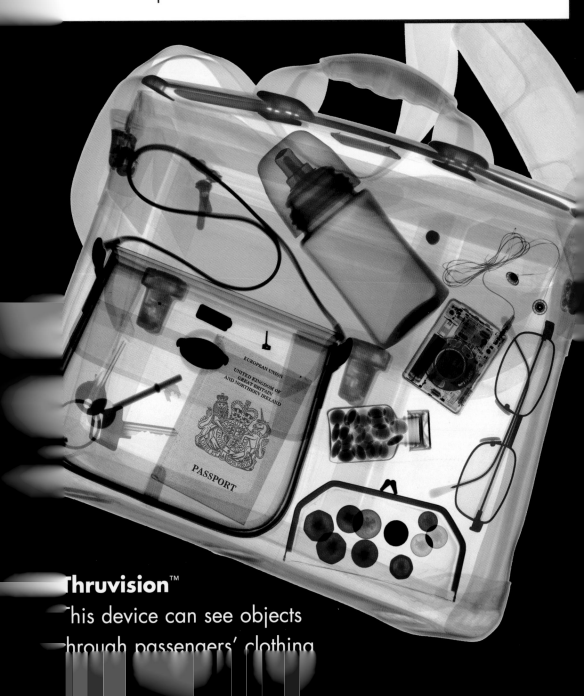

**Thruvision**™
This device can see objects through passengers' clothing

## Imaging technology

This is like an X-ray for people, but instead of showing just a skeleton, it displays the passenger with his or her skin on. Imaging technology can detect whether someone is carrying a weapon or other dangerous item on his or her body.

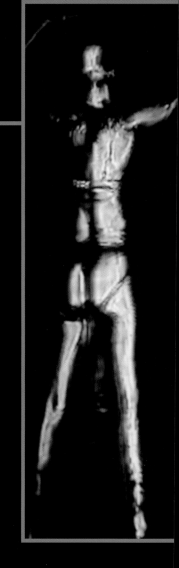

## Explosives trace portals

These machines blow air onto passengers. They then analyze the air for explosives. These machines can detect if a person has been working with or around explosive materials.

*explosives trace portal*

# SURVEILLANCE

**CCTV cameras are everywhere. There are 4.2 million cameras just in the United Kingdom alone! That is a fifth of all the CCTV cameras in the world. No one knows for sure how many are in the United States.**

The cameras send images to monitors, where police watch to see if someone is breaking the law.

In **surveillance**, facial-recognition cameras can recognize and pick out a face from a crowd—perhaps a criminal on the run.

Police watch crowds using "drones." Drones are small remote-controlled helicopters fitted with CCTV cameras. A drone is 3.2 feet (one meter) wide and weighs about two pounds (0.9 kilograms).

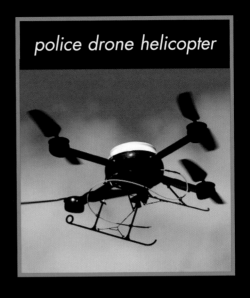

*police drone helicopter*

# SPY PLANES

The United States Army use remote-controlled spy planes to ensure certain areas are safe. They are called unmanned aerial vehicles (UAVs).

## MQ-1 Predator

- function: surveillance and **reconnaissance**
- wingspan: 48.5 feet (14.8 meters)
- length: 26.9 feet (8.22 meters)
- weight: 1,128 pounds (512 kilograms)
- speed: 134.8 miles per hour (217 kilometers per hour)
- range: up to 453.6 miles (730 kilometers)
- cameras: three, including one infrared camera

## Wasp III

- function: low-altitude surveillance
- wingspan: 28.5 inches (72.3 centimeters)
- length: ten inches (25.4 centimeters)
- weight: 15.9 ounces (450 grams)
- speed: between 19.8 and 39.7 miles per hour (32 and 64 kilometers per hour)
- cameras: two day/night cameras

# CREDIT CARDS

**Credit card theft is a big problem.**

People often steal credit cards or copy the cards' details. They can then use the cards to buy items online, over the phone, or by mail. They do not need a card's PIN to do this.

A new card hopes to put an end to credit card theft. The Emue card has its own display screen and keypad.

When you type your PIN into the card, it displays a new number. Without this number, the card is useless. It comes up with a different number every time, so only the PIN holder can use it.

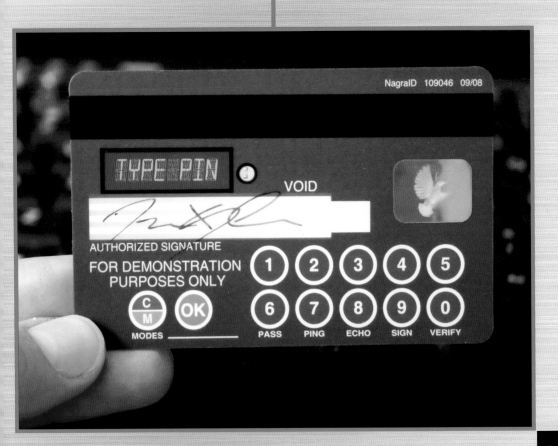

# BODYGUARDS

**Close protection officers (CPOs) are specially trained to physically protect people from harm.**

World leaders often have a small army of CPOs to protect them against people who may wish to cause him or her harm.

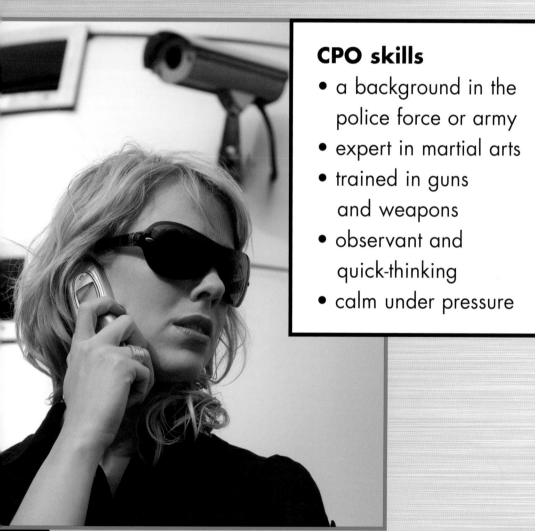

## CPO skills
- a background in the police force or army
- expert in martial arts
- trained in guns and weapons
- observant and quick-thinking
- calm under pressure

## CPO gadgets
- a non-lethal weapon
- baton, pepper spray, and electric stun gun
- defensive flashlight that contains a defensive device, such as pepper spray
- bulletproof vest
- **covert** earpiece and radio set
- Tuff-writer™ defensive pen—writes under the most extreme conditions and can be used as a defensive weapon
- handcuffs

# FORT KNOX

**Fort Knox, in Kentucky, is the most secure building in the world. It is a** fortress **protected by a state-of-the-art security system and armed guards.**

Inside the building is a vault containing billions of dollars in U.S. government gold bars.

The vault is lined with granite walls and a door weighing more than 20 tons (18.14 metric tons).

No visitors are allowed inside the vault.

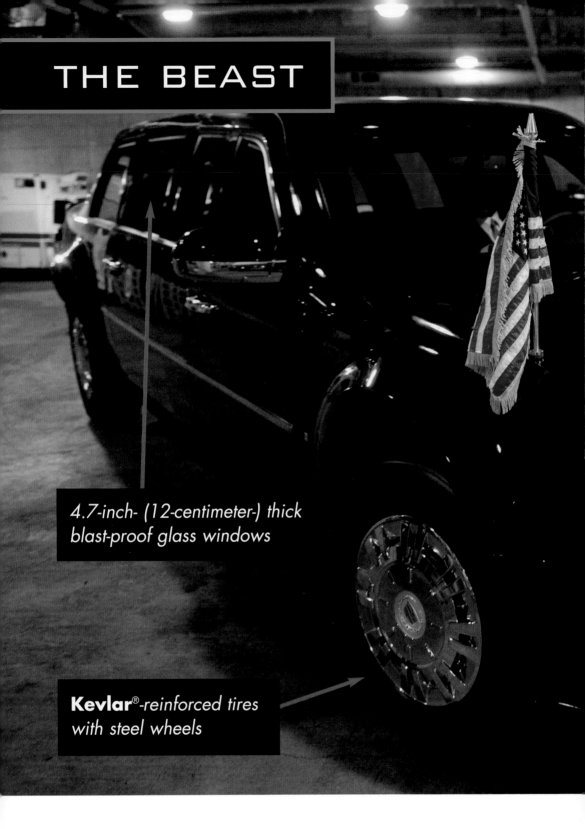

# THE BEAST

*4.7-inch- (12-centimeter-) thick blast-proof glass windows*

**Kevlar**®*-reinforced tires with steel wheels*

The U.S. president's limousine is called "The Beast." It is the most advanced and secure protection vehicle in the world.

The vehicle weighs about six tons (5.4 metric tons).

4.7-inch- (12-centimeter-) thick armor plating

armored fuel tank

**Only a few** Secret Service **agents know all of the vehicle's features, and they are sworn to secrecy!**

**biometrics** The process of measuring and storing information about the human body

**closed-circuit television (CCTV)** A system where one or more cameras transmit moving images to monitors

**covert** Not openly shown; covered over

**drawbridge** A bridge that can be raised and lowered

**fortress** A structure built for protection

**infrared** A short wavelength of invisible radiation that can detect heat

**Kevlar**® A human-made fiber of great strength

**moat** A deep ditch surrounding a castle, usually filled with water

**motion sensor** A device that triggers an alarm or light by detecting movement

**reconnaissance** A military operation carried out to observe an area of land in order to locate an enemy

**Secret Service** The U.S. agency that protects current and former presidents

**surveillance** Close observation of a person or people

**Web browser** A program used to access information on the Internet

# DID YOU KNOW?

- The United Kingdom contains one percent of the world's population but has 20 percent of the world's CCTV cameras.

- Biometric security is used at Disneyland® —fingerprint scanners are used at the amusement park to prevent people sharing their admission tickets.

# SECURITY ONLINE

This Web site is designed to teach kids about U.S. homeland security.
*www.fema.gov/kids/nse*

This Web site looks at the different machines used for airport security.
*www.howstuffworks.com/airport-security.htm*

This Web site provides information about the U.S. Secret Service.
*www.secretservice.gov*

This Web site has information about MI5, the agency that protects the United Kingdom against threats to national security.
*www.mi5.gov.uk*

# INDEX